Writing Copy for the Web
in a week

C000091899

NIGEL TEMPLE

Hodder & Stoughton

A MEMBER OF THE HODDER HEADLINE GROUP

Orders: please contact Bookpoint Ltd, 130 Milton Park, Abingdon, Oxon
OX14 4SB.
Telephone: (44) 01235 827720, Fax: (44) 01235 400454. Lines are open from
9.00–6.00, Monday to Saturday, with a 24 hour message answering service.
Email address: orders@bookpoint.co.uk

British Library Cataloguing in Publication Data
A catalogue record for this title is available from The British Library

ISBN 0 340 85802 8

First published 2003
Impression number   10 9 8 7 6 5 4 3 2 1
Year   2007 2006 2005 2004 2003

Cover image: Photodisc/ Getty Images
Typeset by SX Composing DTP, Rayleigh, Essex.
Printed in Great Britain for Hodder & Stoughton Educational, a division of
Hodder Headline Plc, 338 Euston Road, London NW1 3BH. by Cox & Wyman
Ltd, Reading, Berkshire.

chartered
management
institute

inspiring leaders

The leading organisation for professional management

As the champion of management, the Chartered Management Institute shapes and supports the managers of tomorrow. By sharing intelligent insights and setting standards in management development, the Institute helps to deliver results in a dynamic world.

Setting and raising standards

The Institute is a nationally accredited organisation, responsible for setting standards in management and recognising excellence through the award of professional qualifications.

Encouraging development, improving performance

The Institute has a vast range of development programmes, qualifications, information resources and career guidance to help managers and their organisations meet new challenges in a fast-changing environment.

Shaping opinion

With in-depth research and regular policy surveys of its 91,000 individual members and 520 corporate members, the Chartered Management Institute has a deep understanding of the key issues. Its view is informed, intelligent and respected.

For more information call 01536 204222 or visit www.managers.org.uk

CONTENTS

■ I N T R O D U C T I O N ■

Do you own, run or have input into a business website? Do you write, commission or edit any of the words? If the answer is 'Yes' to either or both of these questions, then this book can help you.

Why do customers and prospects visit your site? Why do they return? For a business website, the answer is information. The majority of this information comprises words which we will call 'Web copy'.

We start, on Sunday, with the big picture. We look at why you must think differently, if you are producing words for the Web. On Monday, we consider what to write about – the 'content' as it is known in the trade.

On Tuesday, Web copy style is examined. Although style is a subjective area, we look at the approaches that work well on the internet. On Wednesday, we discuss Web copy structure. Furthermore, we consider how to use your words to sell on the internet.

Thursday is devoted to e-mail marketing. This technique can help to raise awareness of your enterprise and generate more business.

Grammar and vocabulary are looked at on Friday. Many people may not have enjoyed grammar at school, so we will keep this short and to the point!

Finally, on Saturday, we consider writing strategies and editing. You will find that each chapter includes tips and ideas, to make your Web copy more effective.

Within a week, you will know a great deal more about this subject. Just a few of the ideas could make all the difference to the effectiveness of your website. We hope that you enjoy reading this book.

Web copy thinking

Writing for the internet calls for a different way of thinking. Four other forms of mass media preceded the internet:

1 Books
2 Newspapers and magazines
3 Radio
4 TV

The USP of the internet

Until the 21st century, these four types of mass media shared one thing in common: they only offered one-way communication. In other words, you could not communicate back to the author, journalist, broadcaster or company unless you used another medium such as the telephone or the postal service. However, the USP (Unique Selling Proposition) of the internet is that it is *interactive*. This means that, on the internet, your reader can:

- Click on a link
- Forward your copy
- Send an e-mail
- Fill in an interactive form
- Ask for more information
- Place an order

Of course, you can choose to make your words passive. They can just sit there on the internet. However, you would then miss out on one of the great opportunities of 21st century communication: interactive communication with your audience.

The challenges of Web copywriting

Writers everywhere face similar challenges, including:

- Finding enough information and source material
- Keeping motivated
- Time pressures
- Deciding how much to write
- Grappling with grammar
- Overcoming mental blocks

If you have to produce words for the internet, you are faced with additional challenges:

- Should you make your content interactive?
- Is your copy easy to read on-screen?
- Does the sequence work?
- How often do you allow the reader to jump to new information (using hyperlinks)?
- How do you keep your content up to date?
- Is the style right for the internet?
- Will people from different cultures understand you?

This book will help you to deal with these difficulties.

Computer display challenges

The words, numbers, symbols and graphics on computer screens are constantly being 'refreshed'. However, staring at these flickering images for protracted periods can be very tiring. This is why brevity tends to work well on the internet.

Some Web designers favour very small typefaces, which many people find difficult to read. Moreover, all sorts of high-tech wizardry is used on websites, and this can make it more difficult to understand the words.

The way that words are laid out on-screen varies widely. Finding what you want can be very frustrating. To compound the issue, your Web copy will be seen on various screen sizes, with different settings and using different software versions.

Passing traffic

Having a website is similar to owning a shop in a busy high street. There is a constant stream of people passing by outside and a few people decide to pop into your shop. However, most leave without buying anything or without leaving their contact details.

People often visit several websites in one session (just like they visit several stores on a Saturday afternoon). Sadly, they may never visit your website again. It is difficult to achieve website 'brand loyalty'.

Nevertheless, well-written words will encourage visitors to return. If you deliver something special, they will recommend your website to their business contacts. (Word of mouth is one of the best types of marketing).

Being a writer

How much Web copy writing will you actually do? Will you write all of it? If so, you will need to have a firm grasp of your subject matter, a reasonable amount of time to write, a good vocabulary and understanding of grammar; and take pleasure in writing.

Where will all these words come from? If you do not want to do all of the writing, you could:

- Ask other people in your organisation to contribute something. (There's no harm in asking – is there?)
- Borrow some words from your organisation's brochures, other printed matter, press releases and

so on. (Hence the term 'brochureware'. A first generation website is often little more than an electronic version of the company brochure).

- Import content from other websites – with their permission. This is discussed later in the book.
- Hire a professional copywriter. (Not as expensive as you might think).
- Outsource the whole thing to your PR consultancy, if you have one.

If you intend to use these strategies, this book will help you to become a better editor.

Thinking ahead

As with most things in life, planning ahead is the key to success when writing for the internet. There are several key issues to consider.

Where are you heading?
- *What are you trying to achieve with your Web copy?* Put time aside to consider this question carefully. Have a brainstorming session with your colleagues. Decide what you want people to do, once they have read your words. Write down your objectives. Ineffective copywriting – particularly on the internet – is usually the child of poor thinking.
- *How do you want your readers to react?* Unlike other communication media, you can get instant, accurate feedback on what your readers think of your words and what actions, if any, they subsequently take.

- *What are the key messages?* Find a way to talk about them as early as possible. For example:

> This section describes the benefits of joining our organisation. We will look at the available positions, tell you where they are and give you a step-by-step guide for applying on-line.

Focus on your target readership
- *Who are you writing for?* On the internet, this can be a complex question. Unless you use password controls, anyone with internet access and a Web browser has access to your words. The answer is to segment your market and have a clear understanding of who you are writing for. Tip: Write a profile of the type of person you are targeting (individuals read websites, not companies or markets!)
- *Addressing needs*: are you clear about the needs of your internet audience? Have you taken the trouble to try to find out?
- *How do they want the copy presented?* Technical readers may want facts and figures in well-presented formats, whereas passing traffic may need benefits that jump out at them to get them to stop and take a look. Find out what these different needs are by using questionnaires and speaking to a representative sample of your target audience.

Research
- *Where will the source material come from?* How much material can you gather from within your organisation? Will you need additional material from other sources?

Learning to type
- *Can you touch-type?* Or are you a two-fingered typist? If so, keying in will be a lengthy process. Until speech recognition software becomes cheap, easy to use and reliable, the only effective way to get your words into the machine is through the keyboard. However, for a modest investment of time and effort, you can learn to touch-type. There are a number of CD-ROM based products available for learning to type. These are fine if you are reasonably self-disciplined. Alternatively, join a class or get a friend to teach you.

Getting their attention
- *Your first words*: no, not 'Da Da' or 'Ma Ma'. We mean the first words that people read on your website. After all, if you do not grab the reader's attention, they will not read on, will they?

Technically speaking
- *Does your copy have to integrate with other online content?* You need to think about consistency of style, use of navigation, etc.
- *Are there any technical considerations?* Do you need to discuss these with your Web development agency or technical colleagues? It is always best to find out before you put your fingers to the keypad!

Style
- *What style should your Web copy be written in?* This will be covered in detail on Tuesday.

Chronologically speaking
- *Create deadlines*: how much time do you have to produce your Web copy? How many stages are there in the editing process? Professional writers work to deadlines and so should you.

- *When will you get the writing done?* Plan your writing time. Set time aside in your diary. Make this a high priority item because otherwise, 'urgent' work will take over from 'important' work, such as producing Web copy.

Don't disturb! Writer at work!

- *Where will you write?* Is it feasible to write somewhere else instead of at the office? A quiet place to work will make you more productive.

Editing and proofreading

- *Who will edit and proofread your copy?* Never upload Web copy to the internet until someone else has read through it who is good at spelling (do not trust spell checkers). Schedule this as part of the process.

Keeping up to date

Technology is continually changing and you must keep up to

speed with what is happening. This includes developments in software and hardware (i.e. mobile devices which can receive and display your words). Take a look at new websites, subscribe to the high circulation e-zines (e-mail magazines) and buy some internet magazines from your newsagent.

The generosity principle

Like it or loathe it, people expect free stuff on the internet. Many websites have tried (and failed) to launch paid-for content. This situation may change but, for the time being, with so much free content out there, the general feeling is: 'Hey! Why pay if I can use a search engine and find what I want for free?'

This fact of internet life is part of the generosity principle. It is just the way the internet is. However, there is a much better (and more businesslike) reason to consider using this principle in everything you write for the internet.

There are many individuals and organisations with a 'take, take, take' philosophy. They happily take your time, take your money, and take a hike when you need something from them! On the other hand, many others have a different philosophy. They take the time and trouble to get to know you. They are interested and they are good listeners. If there is a problem in the relationship, they sort it out. How does this attitude feel to you?

If you provide useful, free information you will generate more website traffic, get people talking about your website, and create a sense of trust.

How can you apply this principle? You could:

- *Offer a free e-zine (e-mail magazine)*: you can then send regular, relevant and well written e-zines to prospects and customers, which will help to build your brand and give you many marketing opportunities. As well as a great example of interactivity, this simple idea shows that you want to be helpful and proactive in your business relationships. This is a great message, in its own right. You will find detailed information about e-zines in Thursday's chapter on e-mail marketing.
- *Provide informative articles.*
- *Provide hyperlinks to other websites*: this was the original reasoning behind the internet, i.e. a network of interconnected computers, files and resources. Another benefit of this strategy is that certain search engines will rank your site higher if you have numerous external links. Furthermore, many visitors will 'retrace their steps' to get back to a website that you have recommended and, therefore, pass through your website once again. One technical tip for you: ensure that any site that you hyperlink to, kicks into a separate browser window so that the visitor does not lose your website.

All of these ideas can help to deliver more customers, sales and profits.

How do people read websites?

To a very large extent, people do not read websites. Instead, they are used to scanning Web pages – just like newspapers. They jump from headline to headline, with their eye following an 'S' curve, as it scans the screen.

Interestingly, our eyes can only focus on a very small area at any one time. When we read text, we do this in 'chunks'. In other words, we 'input' a few words at a time and then skip on to the next batch of words. We typically do exactly the same thing on a new Web page – we quickly scan the page, picking out headlines, graphics and highlighted items. As we do this, we decide whether we want to read any text in full, jump to a linked page or leave that site altogether.

Therefore, it is very important to learn how professional marketers and advertisers do what they do. They will tell you that you must, firstly, get your reader's attention (with an effective headline and/or a relevant image) and then hold their interest (i.e. long enough to read your copy).

Specifically, you need to tell your audience 'up front' what is in it for them if they take the time to read your brilliant Web copy. You will learn more about this on Wednesday.

Always think in terms of benefits

Everyone is familiar with the concept of benefits. These are the reasons that people buy things and use services, such as websites. However, when you visit a new website, you may often find it difficult to figure out the benefits of the site. What will it do for you? What will you learn? How will your life change for the better, if you stick around?

Think about your website for a moment. Is it clear what the site will deliver? Only providing a list of website features (perhaps in menu form), is not an effective strategy. Consider telling people how they will benefit from reading further, from clicking on that link, or from doing what you want them to do.

Branding

The foundation of any relationship is trust. It is easy to put up a website or launch an e-mail marketing business. Therefore, rapidly establishing your credentials is a key issue. If you work for a large, well-known company, the answer is of course to display your logo and branding on every page of your website. However, what if you are not a 'famous name'? Your Web copy can go a long way to establishing credibility, which is exactly what this book is about!

A global audience

Potentially, people of every nationality are able to look at anything you publish on the internet. Even if you only wish to communicate within a limited geographical market, you must be aware that we live in a multicultural world.

On Tuesday we will look at Web copy style. One of the key messages is to keep everything clear and simple, which is, of course, easier said than done. If you follow this advice, your Web copy will certainly be easier to understand for an international internet audience.

Which websites do you like?

Which business websites do you like the most? Why do you keep returning to them? Ask your colleagues and contacts which sites they like and take a look at these as well. Analyse the content and see what is useful and user-friendly. Start filling a notebook (or use a file on your computer) with notes about what you like/don't like and ideas that you can use in the future.

Think of this as a journey

As we reach the end of Sunday, remember that websites and e-zines are dynamic. It is better to get going, learn from your mistakes and see what works, than to try and get it perfect, first time around. Until you present your Web copy to the ultimate judge – the marketplace – you will not know what the reaction will be. Think of the whole process as a journey, not a destination, and have fun. Words and the internet – what an interesting combination!

Summary

In this chapter, we have looked at how you must change your perspective when you write for the internet. We have looked at the key planning issues and considered how people read websites. Your main focus must be to look at your Web copy from the visitors' perspective.

Web copy content

This chapter looks at the issue of what to write about within your website. It also examines some of the key words that can make all the difference when it comes to convincing your visitors to continue reading.

Gateway pages

Many websites have a 'gateway' page, which appears first. Typically, gateway pages have a company logo with the words 'Enter our website' written underneath. Sometimes they also include other messages or information.

These special pages can be used for search engine optimisation. Some organisations use them as a greetings page, before you get to the homepage proper. However, from the point of view of the visitor, they create another step before they reach your website proper.

The homepage: first impressions

Most visitors will enter your site via your homepage. Remember that you never get a second chance to make a first impression. So, let's think about first impressions for a moment.

What are the first words which appear as your homepage builds? Access your site from someone else's computer, who has not visited your site before. Preferably, choose a computer with a slow connection speed. You will then get a better impression of what the first-time visitor actually experiences.

Did you know that you can specify the order that you want everything to materialise in? A sentence or two describing what your website is all about, would be very useful as the first item that appears.

In many ways, homepages act as an advertisement for the rest of the website. If your advert fails to capture attention and generate interest, visitors will simply melt away. Make it clear who you are and what this site offers. Do not end up with a cluttered layout that makes it difficult to figure out what is available on your website.

Opening words

The first words that the visitor reads are incredibly
important. Here are some options for you:

- The name of your business (or your name).
- 'Welcome to . . .' Ever popular and friendly, but not
  original.
- A question, i.e. 'Are you looking for . . .?' This really
  does turn the homepage into an advert. Questions
  are very effective: the mind will involuntarily answer
  the question (you probably answered that one
  automatically, didn't you?)
- A benefit statement (focused on your product or
  service).
- A one-line description of who you are and what you do.

The next time you surf the internet, think about the first
words that appear at the top of the different homepages.
What works and what does not?

The homepage: organising your content

How to organise your homepage content is one of the hardest
sets of decisions you will have to make concerning your
website. Here are the options facing you:

- Use the homepage as an index page for the rest of
  the site. It will then look like a portal, with dozens of
  organised headings and subheads. All very logical,
  but rather boring to look at.

- Have a large amount of content on your homepage. This scrolls endlessly down and down. Many Web experts use this approach and it works for them.
- Use a hybrid approach. This will include hyperlinks to the main parts of your website. In addition, there will be 'teaser' paragraphs that act as hooks, to try to get the reader to burrow deeper into your site.

Navigation words

Here is a list of the typical navigation items you will find on homepages. Read through it and consider which items would be most useful for your website visitors. In addition, it is recommended that you ask a selection of visitors what they would find useful.

- *About us*: more friendly than 'Corporate Information' or 'Company Profile'. This should be a brief explanation of what you do, what is different/interesting about you, where you are based and other relevant information. Do not assume that everybody knows what you do or what your type of business does. The style here should be informative and factual.
- *Advertise*: once you have built a successful site, it can generate cash via banner ads and other forms of advertising. This is where the visitor will learn how many unique visitors you get every month and the rates you charge.
- *Book shop*: it is easy to become an affiliate with one of the major online bookstores. If visitors jump to their website from your site and order a book, the online bookstore will pay you a commission. In addition, you are offering another useful service to your visitors.

- *Careers*: if you work in an organisation which has job vacancies, why not advertise these on your website?
- *Clients/Customers*: in business, this is a great chance to prove your credibility. For any famous name corporate clients, include their logos for instant recognition. (Ask their permission first, though).
- *Contact us*: this usually comprises a form for you to fill in. The problem with forms is that many people do not like filling them in. Simplify the process (i.e. do not ask for too much information). Furthermore, give enquirers many different ways to contact you (i.e. by e-mail, phone, fax or by writing to your address).
- *Customer/Client service*: if they have a problem, give them plenty of opportunity to tell you about it.
- *Events*: may or may not apply to you. If you include this section, keep it up to date.
- *FAQ*: Frequently Asked Questions. This usually lists all of the questions. Make each question into a hyperlink to take the reader to the relevant answer (lower down the page).
- *Finding us*: obviously, you will provide a map. In addition, provide stab point lists in separate sections for people travelling to you from different directions. Give them clear, step-by-step guidance. It is recommended that you travel this route yourself and check that your directions work in practice. All too often, directions are confusing to follow.
- *Fun stuff*: most people would probably take a look, wouldn't they?
- *Help*: could mean anything, couldn't it? Depending on who you are and what your site is all about, 'Help' could be hints on how to get the best out of your website as well as contact information (including the Webmaster's e-mail address).

- *Hot topics/articles*: this is usually a list of the most frequently read items on your website. You should be able to find this information from your site statistics.
- *Internet shop*: depending on the type of business you are in, you may be able to sell directly from your website, or set up a separate e-commerce site.
- *Legalities*: here you can tell visitors what (if anything) they can copy. If you work for a large organisation, your legal department or advisors will probably want to write this section.
- *Links*: can be very useful. Moreover, many search engines will boost your ratings if you have external links.
- *Members area*: usually accessible only with a password. You must be prepared to keep the content in this section up to date.
- *My account*: strictly for sophisticated websites with serious 'back-end' systems, such as web-enabled databases.
- *News* (i.e. company news): latest updates and developments. Warning: if you have this section, you must keep it up to date.
- *News* (i.e. newspaper news): this can be provided in numerous formats.
- *Newsletter*: if you publish an e-mail newsletter (e-zine), this will be a link to your most recent edition.
- *Newsletter archive*: this is where visitors can find back issues of your e-zines.
- *Partners*: the internet can be a very cooperative place. Why not promote some of your business partners (provided they do the same for you)?
- *Personal*: (for personal/small business sites). This will certainly arouse curiosity.
- *Press room*: 'Media Information' is an alternative. Within

this section, you should have:

- An organisational profile (written for the media, i.e. without superlatives and factually based)
- Profiles of your media spokespersons
- Copies of your press releases, listed in chronological order
- Contact information

- *Pricing*: this will either be up-to-date pricing information or details about your pricing policy.
- *Products/services*: some websites have pages and pages of product/service listings. Think about it from the visitors' viewpoint! How can you simplify and categorise your portfolio of offerings? Try to make the headings visible on one page (without scrolling). In addition, add a search facility.
- *Reports*: if you publish reports, make them available on your website (perhaps for a fee).
- *Resources*: this can be a meaningless word. It could include hyperlinks to other websites, articles, book recommendations or digitalised information products downloads (see page 31).
- *Search*: if you end up with a large website, offer a search facility. Various search engines allow you to add their technology to your site (some for free, some for a fee). Visitors should be able to search within your site, by entering search words into a rectangular 'field' and clicking 'go'. Of course, you can allow them to search the entire World Wide Web as well!
- *Site map*: very useful on big sites. Could comprise section headings and subheads or it could be a Mind Map® (please refer to *Mind Maps® in a week* by Steve Morris and Jane Smith).

- *Survey*: why not ask visitors to fill in an online survey concerning your products, services, company or other issue? You never know what you might learn.
- *Tips and ideas*: useful, customer-focused information. Within this section, ask visitors to e-mail you with their tips and hints (if you decide to publish their responses, ask for their permission first).
- *Testimonials*: a very important part of the sales process and often left out of websites – pat yourself on the back if you have them.

On other pages, you will need:

- *Home*: this is fine, an alternative is the word 'Homepage'.

Articles

Your website is a great place to publish articles. These could include:

- Technical articles about aspects of your products or services.
- 'How to' articles focusing on how to solve problems. These can refer to your products or services.
- Business articles, which describe aspects of your business and the benefits of using your business, etc.
- Case studies – stories written about happy customers or clients who have benefited from using your products or services. Do not forget that testimonial statements are like gold dust. Scatter these liberally around your website – they are good for credibility.

The articles may be written specifically for your website or they may be edited versions of articles you have used elsewhere. Remember to clear case studies with everyone concerned.

You are about to become a self publisher, but you should still exercise some restraint. Tuesday covers this in more detail.

Forms

The USP of the internet is its interactivity. Forms are a great way to get people to interact with you and it is worth the effort to get them right.

Keep website forms short and simple. The basic rule is that the more information you ask for, the fewer the responses you will get back. After all, do you like filling in forms?

Think hard about what you absolutely must know, before you produce a form. Here is a typical website form:

Full name:

E-mail:

Phone:

Comment:

Address:

Why is 'Full name' asked for? Do they want your middle name if you have one? In a multicultural society, 'First name' and 'Surname' are better as separate fields. As a secondary point, some questions may not line up with the field, which is a problem with the table layout. Tables are useful to line up text on a website; however, this is a fiddly job which has to be done correctly.

Asking for an e-mail address is fine. Many people have several e-mail addresses and this gives them a chance to choose the most appropriate one.

Then we have 'Phone'. Why would anyone want to give out their phone number, particularly if the site has not breathed a word about its privacy policy?

'Comment' is acceptable. Nevertheless, think about the nature of the form and the type of feedback you are looking for. Whichever word you choose will predispose people to give you different types of feedback. Alternatives are: 'Your message', 'Feedback' and 'Question'.

The same issues that apply to 'Phone' may arise with 'Address'.

Finally, you must decide which fields (if any) will be mandatory and must, therefore, be filled in. Normal practice is to mark these with an asterisk and note that these are mandatory.

Privacy statements

Increasingly, website visitors are wary about giving contact information. They do not want to find their e-mail inboxes cluttered with messages from you – or, even worse, that you have sold their details to third parties.

Whenever you ask for contact information, state your privacy policy loud and proud. Here are two options:

1 The word 'Privacy' is displayed as a hyperlink (usually in red). The link takes you to a separate page, which describes your privacy policy in detail. For example, where a site is soliciting e-zine subscriptions:

> **PRIVACY POLICY**
> Your data is private. We won't pass it on or sell it to anyone else. You can always unsubscribe, by sending an e-mail to ezine@the-entirely-trustworthy-internet-shop-i-mean-would-i-lie-to-you.com with the word 'unsubscribe' in the subject line.

2 Alternatively, you can write a sentence which gets the gist
   of this across. For example:

> *Privacy: We will never disclose your details to anyone else*

Display this message whenever you ask people to
subscribe to your e-mail e-zine or whenever they are filling
in a form. You should then get a higher response rate.

Photograph captions

As a general rule, caption all of the photographs that appear
within your website. Captions should be factual and they
should fit underneath the photo, on one line. It is fine to use a
small typeface (a ten-point font is suitable). Please refer to
'Rollovers' on page 48.

Quoting your sources

Quoting your sources will earn more credibility and trust.
Tell your readers where your information and statistics come
from. In addition, you may wish to provide hyperlinks to
websites that contain source information.

Digitised information products

A digitised information product is useful information
provided in electronic form. You can produce this as a plain
text e-mail, an html e-mail, a file attachment (e.g. a word
processed document) or as an Adobe® PDF file. The latter

ensures that the document will look the way you want it to when it is viewed; you can disable the 'copy' and 'print' options if you wish. Examples of information products include:

- A 'How to' guide
- Tips and hints
- Do's and don'ts

For instance, if you provide a service, you could write a short guide on choosing a supplier for your type of service. You could then offer this on your website for free, in exchange for contact information.

Alternatively, you could provide a guide on how to get the best out of your product or service. These items are usually offered for free. If executed properly, they can generate substantial word-of-mouth marketing for you, as well as more sales enquiries.

The information product can be read onscreen or printed out. If you wish, hyperlinks can be provided for more in-depth information. Here are some writing tips for information products:

- Begin with a description of what lies ahead
- Include some benefits in this description, i.e. 'Learn how to . . .'
- Give plenty of examples and tell stories so that readers can visualise what you mean
- Provide check-lists – if appropriate
- Remember to include all of your contact information

Imported content

If you import content from another website, you can avoid writing altogether – at least for that bit, anyway!

There are several ways to do this. However, you must ask the other website owner's permission (and get this in writing). Besides the legal ramifications, you can be sure that people who copy other people's words and content without permission will be found out!

1 Many websites offer free content to other websites. Good examples include various newspapers and a number of specialist 'newsfeed' providers. To find an up-to-date list, key in 'content providers' or 'free content' in a search engine.
You can visit the content provider's website and register. Some lines of HTML (Hyper Text Markup Language – the computer language of the internet) will be displayed for you (or your web technicians) to copy and insert into your website.
Once you have done this (and uploaded the changes to your website hosting service), then the relevant content/links will appear within your website.

2 Look out for interesting articles and content as you cruise around the World Wide Web. If you find an interesting item, you can e-mail the author or Webmaster and ask whether you can publish it on your website. People are usually happy to say yes, provided that the article is attributed to them and perhaps a hyperlink is inserted for their website.

3 Another idea is to form alliances with other organisations (who do not compete with you) and swap content. Due to the very nature of the internet, they could be on the other side of the world. Find some well-written websites and send them an exploratory e-mail.

4 Of course, if all else fails, you could pay someone to do the writing for you. There are many excellent freelancer writers and they are not typically very expensive generally. If you work for a company, this is certainly one route that you may wish to explore.

Metatags

Sorry, but we have to get a little technical here! Metatags are words which help certain search engines to classify your website. Please note that not all search engines use Metatags.

Metatags are contained within the HTML, at the top of many homepages (and quite often, other pages too).

- *Title tags*: the title tag is found near the top of the HTML of every web page. It generates the strapline that appears at the top of your browser window.
  Create a different title tag for each and every page on your website. This will make your site look more professional – and help you in the search engine ranking battle.
- *Description tag*: the description tag produces a description of the page in place of the summary that the search engine would create. In effect, this should look like a headline for an advert. People will skip down the search engine rankings so your description tag has to jump out at them.

It is worth thinking long and hard about the words you use – test out variations on your target audience.

- *Keywords tags*: some search engines 'spider' your site and go through your keywords. When someone uses a search engine, it refers back to these keywords. If you have them, you can see them by 'right clicking' with your PC mouse (on a homepage – once your cursor is hovering over a blank part of the page). Now select 'View Source'. No keyword tags? They may be 'cloaked'. Try another site.

Here is the HTML from the top of my website homepage (www.nigeltemple.com):

```
<html>
<head>
<title>Nigel Temple: Free marketing ideas, tips and articles</title>
<meta name="description" content="Discover a treasure trove of FREE
marketing articles, ideas and advice.">
<meta name="keywords" content="nigel temple, marketing, marketing
advice, marketing consultancy, marketing ideas, marketing training,
marketing speaker, public speakers, creative thinking, mind maps, mind
mapping">
```

Notice that each Metatag is separated by a comma. Also notice different ways that people might search for a subject (e.g. 'mind maps' and 'mind mapping') are included. Some people also include common spelling variations.

If you want to learn more about Metatags, visit: www.searchenginewatch.com. This is a complex and ever-changing area. There are now many companies that offer help with search engine ranking. In addition, you can buy software (such as Webposition Gold®: www.webposition.com), which can help you with Metatags and search engine submission.

Incidentally, search engines love plain text pages, packed full of Web copy. If your site is full of graphics and has relatively little text, the search engines will not love you!

As you may have discovered, keeping up with the search engines can become a full-time job. However, getting the Metatags right is well worth the effort.

Summary

Today, we have explored the main components of a website. We have discussed the need to make a strong first impression and you now have a check-list of content areas (presented as navigation words). We have also talked about privacy, imported content and the technical area of Metatags.

Web copy style

This chapter examines the golden rules of internet writing style. The pros and cons of different styles will be discussed. We will also look at presentation details, such as typefaces, colour and emphasis.

Begin with clear thinking

As we discussed on Sunday, clear thinking leads to clear writing. Are you clear about:

- Your objectives?
- Who you are writing for?
- Your subject matter?

Make it personal

Think of someone who is typical of the audience you are trying to reach. Ideally, this is someone you know personally. If this is not possible, create an image of someone who typifies your target audience.

When you write, imagine that you are having a conversation with that person. Write down the words that come to mind in this imaginary conversation. Keep thinking about this individual, their situation and their needs. This approach will give your words a more intimate, personal feeling.

Focus on the reader

When you are producing Web copy, focus on the person you

are conversing with, i.e. the reader. Use the word 'You' as much as possible, but do not use the words 'I' and 'We' so often.

A good test is to go through paragraphs or sections of your Web copy and count the number of times you have used these three words. Try and use 'You' four times as often as you use 'I' and 'We'. When people read your Web copy, it will come over as much more personal and engaging as a result.

Be concise

By being concise, you show that you care about your website visitors' time. You demonstrate that you do not want to waste their time. However, being concise can be hard work; you will have to put in the extra effort to edit and polish your Web copy.

Your Web copy will automatically be easier to read if it is concise. This means that visitors will be more likely to keep reading. There are three rules for writing readable Web copy:

1 Use short words
2 Use short sentences
3 Use short paragraphs

Vocabulary is covered on Friday but for now, let's just say that short, simple words are best. Remember that you do not have to display your vast vocab on the internet.

Short sentences

According to legend, the editor of a famous tabloid newspaper told his journalists to write sentences that were no more than eight words long. If you try to do this, you will find out how hard it is. An average of 12 words per sentence is recommended. Simply being aware of sentence length will help you to be more concise.

Please refer to page 93 to find out how to cut down sentence length.

Short paragraphs

Each paragraph should be capable of standing alone. It should cover a single point. Imagine a reader copying one of your paragraphs and pasting it into a document. How would it read? Would it make sense?

How long should the ideal paragraph be? Well, if each sentence is 12 words long, then three sentences would give you 36 words. This forms quite a nice, brief paragraph (this paragraph is 36 words long).

Again, just by being aware of the issue, you are more likely to produce punchy paragraphs.

With the exception of very detailed pages, everything should be kept short and to the point. This is because eight out of ten people scan a PC screen rather than read it properly. Why?

- People do not like having to scroll down long pages. They prefer to interact by clicking and moving around the page.
- People do not have the time and they do not want to work hard to get information.
- Reading from PC screens takes longer than reading from paper (it is about 25 per cent slower).
- Looking at a computer screen is more uncomfortable than reading from paper.

Web copy length

How long should your Web copy be? The best answer is to look at the issue from a marketer's perspective. Here is a question for you: 'What is the purpose of marketing?'

The purpose of marketing is to deliver *customers*. However, before anyone can become a customer, they must be made aware of your products, services or business. On the internet, you can boost awareness through search engine positioning, banner advertising and e-mail marketing.

Nevertheless, the majority of people who see your promotional material or who visit your website, will not be in the market for your products or services that day. In fact, probably 90 per cent of people fall into this category. The good news is that some 10 per cent are, therefore, in the market. In other words, they are actively looking for your type of offering.

From a marketing perspective, your Web copy does two jobs at once. Firstly, it creates awareness. The more awareness you generate, the more likely it is that people will come to you when they are in the market. Secondly, it talks to prospective customers who are actively looking for your type of product or service.

This explains why long Web copy works. At this stage of the buying cycle, prospective customers ('prospects') are typically hungry for information. Therefore, many will be very happy to read your Web copy from one end to the other.

Be factual

Providing facts helps to improve belief in your claims. It is
best to be precise, for example:

> - We have 27 clients
> - You can improve performance by an average of
>   26 per cent
> - Learn 16 ways to boost productivity

You may wish to provide hyperlinks to give the reader
further details.

Use of humour

It is fine to sprinkle a little humour around your Web copy.
After all, the internet is a modern, relaxed place. It tends to
be used perhaps by educated people (who enjoy a joke, just
like anyone else).

However, here are some words of warning. Remember that
your sense of humour may not appeal to everybody, so tone
it down a little. Moreover, the internet is accessed by people
from widely different cultural backgrounds. Thus, they may
not get the joke.

Can you think of any brands which incorporate humour? At
any one time, there are always marketing campaigns which
do this effectively.

Most large corporations shy away from any form of humour
on their websites. This is a pity because humour can be a
great way to communicate with people.

Politeness

Politeness works on the internet. Thank people for reading your material. Thank them for filling in a form. Thank them for subscribing to your e-mail e-zine.

Whenever someone sends you an e-mail about your website (regardless of what they are saying), you could begin your response with the words:

> Thank you for your e-mail.

Part of politeness is being prompt. Try your best to get back to people on the same day that they e-mail you. If you cannot do this, try to set up an Autoresponder, to let people know when you will be back at your desk.

Gender

Be politically correct on the internet. If you are not, people will notice. This can lead to negative word-of-mouth publicity and all sorts of knock-on effects.

To keep typing in 'he or she' can become very tedious. The simplest answer may be to use the third person singular – 'you' – whenever you can. In other words, write your Web copy as if you are talking to an individual person (which of course you are).

Be positive

Positive, upbeat Web copy sets a positive, upbeat tone for

your website. It also helps to turn prospects into buyers. If you help people to feel good when they visit your website, they are much more likely to return.

Conversely, handle negativity in your Web copy with care. It can be confusing for the reader.

Menus

In the early 1980s, some of the first PCs came into the UK marketplace. They had green screens, cost about £6000 and had 8-inch floppy discs.

After you had cranked the handle and ignited your Personal Computer, a bright green menu would appear on the screen. Typically, it would list between six and ten options for you to choose between. Each one was numbered; all you had to do was press the relevant number and, hey presto, your application would appear on screen (although you probably had to fiddle around with those floppy discs first).

Today, computers still use menus. Of course, the screens are bigger, the display is in colour and we now have the internet. But it is still menus all the way. The problem is that menu choices on a website screen are typically overwhelming. There is a danger that you will confuse people if you give them too much choice. Therefore, the first issue is clarity.

There are as many design options as there are designers. However, let's look at a straightforward design. This is optimised for Web copy display:

Your Logo   **Company Name**   **Unique Selling Proposition**

Home   **About Us**   **Products**   **Press Room**   **Contact Us**   **FAQ**   **Fun**

◆ *Item one*

◆ *Item two*

◆ *Item three*

◆ *Item four*

◆ *Item five*

◆ *Item six*

◆ *Item seven*

◆ *Item eight*

◆ *Item nine*

[Company name] is the UK's leading supplier of xyzxyz xyz xyzxyz xyzxyz xyz. Xyzxyz xyz xyzxyz xyzxyz xyz.

Are you looking for xyzxyz xyz xyzxyz xyzxyzxy xyz xyzxyz xyz xyzxyz xyzxyz xyzxyz xyzxyz . . . [*more*]

Here is a great story about one of our customers who used our product to . . . [*more*]

News
We have just. launched . .

This approach will load quickly. As you look at the above layout, what do you see first? Take a moment to think about this (by all means jot your answers down).

Most people see the top line. In effect, this is like the headline on an advertisement. From a branding point of view, it is important to keep showing your logo and company name. Notice that the company's USP (Unique Selling Proposition) is included.

Seven items are used from Monday's 'Navigation words' list (page 23). These items form the main menu, strung horizontally across the page. These should be repeated on every page within the website, but not necessarily at the top of the page – they could be little hyperlinks at the bottom of the page.

There is also a set of hyperlinks over to the left (Item one, Item two etc). These will be site-specific items and are set out as a list. This is acceptable provided that the list does not go on for ever!

Typography

- *Fonts*: choose fonts (typefaces) such as Arial, which are easy to read on-screen. Whichever typeface or typefaces you choose, be consistent. Stick with one typeface throughout your website. However, you can use another font for material that you want to stand out on its own. If you use different typefaces, they should have a meaning.
- *Font size*: consistency is the watchword here. Bear in mind that the larger the font size, the less information you can fit on a single screen.
  With regard to font sizes for the body copy (i.e. the main text) on a website, a ten-point font is fine. If you go too small, many people will be unable to read it easily.
- *Case*: originally, when everything on the internet was displayed in plain text, WRITING IN UPPER CASE MEANT THAT YOU WERE SHOUTING. Or if the sender was not raising their virtual voice, at least it denoted emphasis. Now that we have graphics, colour and access to virtually any font we want, we can emphasise without using upper case.
  However, many people use upper case indiscriminately. Advertising professionals will tell you that upper case is more difficult to read than lower case text. This is why newspaper headlines use lower case – if there is a newspaper

to hand take a look. More important stories are simply given a bigger font (i.e. for the story on the front page).

- *Leading capitals*: this issue is enough to drive you mad. Why write 'world' as 'World'? I know it is important, but it is not a name. Please Do Not Use Leading Capitals Indiscriminately. When can you use them? You can use them in headings and headlines, thus:

How to Write Headlines

Note that the preposition 'to' is not honoured with a leading capital.

- *Colour*: too much colour can be confusing. With regard to website text, you may wish to colour code your headlines. If you do, ensure that you are consistent. Also, make sure that the headline colour works well against the background. Quite often, text is difficult to read on websites, because of the strange choice of text and background colours.

- *Emboldening*: in theory, emboldened key words and phrases allow people to scan the page and easily pick out the key points. This is all very well if you use it sparingly; however, too much emboldening makes the text difficult to read. The same point goes for the use of italics.
- *Underlining*: on the internet underlining can look like a hyperlink! The best advice is to steer clear of it.
- *Moving text*: if your web designer likes moving text, beware! It is true that the eye is drawn to movement. The reason being deep-seated survival instincts – if it moves, it might mean danger. The problem is that if you look at any screen with moving images or text for more than a few seconds, the movement can be very distracting.

With text, one popular way to animate it is to use a scrolling 'Marquee'. If you visit a website and see a line of text appearing and then moving across the screen, this is probably done using a Marquee. To get around the annoyance problem, why not scroll the text once and then halt it? You benefit from the drama of movement, but do not annoy people. Other technical tricks, such as animated GIF images and animated Java applets need to be handled with care.

Rollovers

Some web designers use 'rollovers'. These look rather like floating captions and appear as a rectangle, containing text. They materialise when your mouse hovers over an item, such as a graphic or a photograph. If your designer uses these, check them carefully – there are many examples of strange wording inside these text boxes.

Summary

At the end of the day, style is a subjective area. Everyone likes different styles of music and styles of clothes. On the internet, the primary issue is to communicate effectively. If it is difficult to read your text on screen or you have a zany writing style, which is difficult to understand, you will put many people off.

At the same time, to stand out we must adhere to our values and we probably do not want to be bland and boring. A little fun and humour, for example, can certainly enhance your Web copy style.

Today, we have explored various issues surrounding style on the internet. The tips have included communicating with an individual who represents your target audience and the importance of brevity. We have looked at the need for politeness and considered the use of humour. We have also considered style details, such as typography.

Web copy structure and using your Web copy to sell

Structure

When business words are produced in other media, for instance slide presentations, reports or brochures, the material is constructed in sequence. There is a logical progression: a beginning, a middle and an end.

On the internet, the visitor can hop, skip and jump in any order they wish. The question is: Can you have a structure on the Web? Some of the challenges you face include:

- Due to the ability to hyperlink, the notion of sequence is in danger of going out of the window.
- You have little or no control of the path that the visitor takes through your site.
- Someone may forward one of your website pages to a colleague. They decide to visit your site – entering via the page which they have been forwarded.
- Search engines can point people at any page on your site that contains the words they are searching for.
- As websites grow, the visitor may have no idea that certain sections exist.
- Some people do not like scrolling down long pages; they prefer a 'screen at time', with a hyperlink to the next screen of information.
- Other people prefer to scroll as they read.

Clear objectives help to formulate structure

The answer to structure lies in thinking clearly about your objectives before you begin to write the Web copy itself (see Sunday). You must decide what your website is trying to deliver and this objective will guide your decisions on structure.

What is the principle objective of your website? Take a moment to write it in this box:

```



```

You should be able to do this in one or two sentences.

It is quite rare for anyone to answer this question clearly and precisely. Typical responses include:

- 'To build our brand'
- 'To create more awareness'
- 'To generate sales leads'
- 'To act as a resource for our customers'
- 'To be an instance source of information about us'

Of course, you could apply any of these generalisations to any promotional tool. When you think about the objectives for your website, do not be vague. Be specific. For example: 'Our website will help to build brand awareness by having X unique visitors each month. In addition, we expect Y sales leads to come from the site each month.'

Having done this exercise, review your website plan or the website itself and consider whether your structure and content are in line with your stated objectives.

Finding out what your visitors want

A key reason why so many websites fail to deliver is that the companies have not done their research. If you do not know what your readers want you to write about, holding their attention is going to be a tough job.

Produce a mock-up and show it to people

If you are launching a new website, produce a mock-up and show it to your colleagues, customers and contacts. They will undoubtedly give you plenty of feedback on the structure of your website! Incidentally, you can do exactly the same thing, if you are re-launching a website.

Getting their attention

Your first task is to seize the reader's attention. Having achieved this, you must then keep hold of it. As all writers know, this is easier said than done.

From a Web copy structure perspective, begin by telling the audience what is in it for them. A classic method for achieving this is as follows:

Begin by giving the reader some good reasons for keeping on reading. Focus on benefits and needs. Although this may be a fairly obvious statement, few websites do this effectively.

They do not arrest the visitor's attention. This explains why many visitors do not get beyond the homepage.

Give the big picture

Another tip is to give the visitor the big picture of what lies ahead. This is a fundamental need for about two-thirds of the human race. It is all to do with the right side of the brain, which processes images and sees the interconnectedness of things. The right brain needs to see a map of what lies ahead – it wants to see an agenda and it craves for the big picture.

As you cruise the internet, consider the homepages you wander past. Many of us have visited websites and muttered: 'Huh? What is this all about?' Then there are those countless 'me too', undifferentiated, unfocused websites, which fail to communicate a clear benefit of investigating further.

Navigation

As discussed, it is difficult (if not impossible) to foresee which path your visitors will take through your website. Each and every page of your site must, therefore, contain some form of navigation.

At a minimum, you need to have a 'Home' button on each page. 'Contact us', 'Products/Services' and 'Site map' are examples of navigation buttons or hyperlinks that could also appear on every page.

Handling hyperlinks

Hyperlinks are one of the best features of the internet. You can turn any part of your Web copy into a hyperlink. However, it is very easy to get carried away with hyperlinks. The message is to use hyperlinks with discretion.

Text hyperlinks are like signposts – they tell you what to expect if you click on them. On this basis, a text hyperlink can be one word, several words or a sentence. There are various uses for hyperlinks:

- To jump down the page. A typical example would be within a FAQ page. At the top of the page there is a list of FAQs, each of which is hyperlinked to the relevant section or paragraph beneath.
- To jump to another page on your website.
- To jump to another site altogether.
- To jump to your site from another website.
- To jump to your site from an e-mail.

However you use them, test the hyperlink to ensure that it actually works. By the way, if you have inserted a hyperlink yourself, use another machine to test the link – better to be safe than sorry.

Here are some hyperlink tips:

- Hyperlinks should appear in a consistent colour
- Consider using a different font for hyperlinks (particularly in menus)
- Use at least an eight-point typeface for hyperlinks

- As you expand your site, check that the hyperlinks still work
- In a menu, insert a symbol at the start of each separate hyperlink (otherwise the separate hyperlinks can blend into one another)

Search engines and external hyperlinks

One of the original visions of the internet was that it would create a global, interconnected community. This vision is reflected by the fact that certain search engines will rank you higher, if you have external links.

Using summaries

Throughout your website, it is a good idea to use summary paragraphs. These act as 'advertisements' for the next section of text.

Headlines

As discussed previously, you never get a second chance to make a first impression. The headline acts as a gateway to the rest of your text. If the reader's curiosity is not aroused by the headline, they will not read any further. The key is to spend a great deal of time working on your headlines.

The majority of your visitors will scan your Web copy, and so getting the right headlines is critical. Produce a variety of headlines, ask other people for their opinions and, if possible, test different headlines to see which ones get the best reactions.

Subheads

Remember that people typically scan the internet – jumping from one heading to the next. Therefore, use plenty of subheads to break up your Web copy.

Ensure that all of your headlines and subheads transmit a clear meaning. Avoid using complex language and humour in both headlines and subheads, and avoid giving several meanings. Clear signposting is what it is all about.

Bullet points

Bullet points are a good way to display information on the internet:

- ◆ Use them liberally . . .
- ◆ . . . whenever you have a series of points to make
- ◆ On-screen, they are easy on the eye

Print it out, before you upload

Print out each page before you upload it to the internet. The correct way to do this is from within a browser window – you will then see what the reader will see.

Style sheets

Are you looking after your own website? Do you have any Web copy that you want to repeat in different areas of your website? For example, copyright information or a standard menu bar? A little tip, which might save you time and trouble, is to use style sheets. They enable you to change typographical properties without having to go through websites page by page. Most website development packages have them.

Use your Web copy to sell

When it comes to selling and the internet, there are two options. You can use your website to support the sales process or you can attempt to sell directly from your website.

In both cases, you need to be aware that before someone becomes a customer, they go through a buying process. We will use the AIDA model to demonstrate this process.

The AIDA model

AIDA stands for Awareness, Interest, Desire and Action. It is the process that converts a prospect into a customer. If you think in terms of this model, it will act as a guide for the production of your sales-orientated Web copy.

Awareness

If prospective customers are not aware of your glorious website, they will not visit it. You must promote it both on- and off-line. Here are some Web copy related ways to do this.

One of the central messages of this book is that useful, customer-focused, well-written Web copy attracts visitors to websites. Besides your own website, where else can you publish your Web copy? Here are two ideas:

1 *Other websites*: contact the Web masters of non-competing websites and tell them that you have some relevant content. Would they be interested in publishing it? If they are, ask them to put a hyperlink back to your website.
2 *Micro websites*: consider creating a 'micro website'. This could focus on one product or service or a set of products or services. This strategy will mean that you can be more focused with your search engine positioning strategies and other online (and off-line) marketing ideas. It will also give you a splendid platform to display focused Web copy.

You will find many other ways of creating awareness for your site in *Web Marketing in a week* by J. Jonathan Gabay. Within the context of using Web copy to sell, we must consider banner ads, headlines and hyperlinks.

Banner ads and headlines
Banner ads suffered a dramatic decline in revenue and interest, following the dot.com meltdown in 2000. However, they are still a primary way to create online awareness. Banner ads do not have to be the classic rectangular shape. In fact, they can be any shape you like – as long as they are recognisable for what they are.

You are limited for space on a banner ad and so your copy must act like a headline in an advertisement. It must communicate a benefit or proposition to the passing viewer. The best way of doing this is to:

- Brainstorm for key words that focus on the benefit or proposition you offer
- Write at least 12 varieties of headline
- Ask as many people (who match your target audience profile) as possible which headlines they like the best
- Include the words 'click here' within the banner – an obvious call to action, which is often overlooked
- By all means animate your words (or a graphic), however, use animation that kicks into life occasionally – there is nothing more annoying than a constantly moving graphic on a Web page

Hyperlinks

With regards to using Web copy to sell, write benefit-loaded sentences, where space permits. For example:

- 'Products' becomes: 'Learn more about how our products can benefit you'
- 'Customers' becomes: 'Read how our customers have saved money'

One word of warning – do not use hyperlinks in critical selling passages. The reader may click on the link and never return!

Interest

Propositions create interest. A classic internet proposition is 'something for free'. For instance:

- Free 'Tips and Hints' e-book
- Free e-zine
- Free in-depth articles
- Free information
- Free trial

Other propositions include online tools, for example:

- 'Click here to use our on-line price calculator'

Another enduring way to generate interest is to use testimonial statements. People are always interested to find out what other people, who are similar to them, are up to.

Desire

Desire is built by creating a vision of how the visitor can benefit from using your product or service. Desire is founded on trust in your name, brand and website. Famous name brands use testimonials and case studies to prove their credibility and so should you.

Summarising benefits
This is the stage to summarise those benefits. Remind the visitor about all the good things that will happen if they proceed. One way to do this on a Web page is to list the benefits and turn them into hyperlinks. The links take you to a benefit paragraph further down the page.

Getting your reader into 'Yes' mode
Good salespeople know that if they can get a prospective customer to start saying 'Yes' early in the conversation, they are more liable to close the sale.

You can use this concept to your advantage within your Web copy. All you have to do is start using 'Yes Tags'. For example, if it is very cold outside and you say to someone: 'It's really cold today, isn't it?' they are likely to agree with you. Use the same technique in your Web copy. For example: 'Wouldn't it be useful to have all of this information stored on your computer, in an easy-to-use e-book?' Most readers will automatically find themselves agreeing with this statement.

Action

When it comes to calls to action, there are three rules:

1 Do not forget to spell out what you want the visitor to do
   next
2 Give the visitor several ways of contacting you
3 Make it easy for the visitor to do business with you

Once you have constructed the relevant screens, watch a
number of people interact with them before you 'go live'. Do
not say anything to these people while they are trying to
figure out what to do next. You may be surprised at what
they do.

Summary

Today we have looked at the paradox of structure on
websites. The challenge is that if visitors can jump around so
much, can you have structure on a website? We have also
discussed selling on the internet using the AIDA model.

Web copy for e-mail marketing

E-mails can be used to create – and keep – customers.
However, as you will see, there are lots of do's and don'ts in
this area.

E-zines

E-zines (e-mail magazines) are e-mails that are sent to a
group of people. Their e-mail addresses are stored in a
circulation list. In terms of the promotional mix, e-zines
belong to the direct marketing family. There are two types of
e-zine:

1 Permission marketing
2 Spam

Permission marketing
If someone gives you consent to send them your e-zine, this
is called permission marketing. The guru in this area is Seth
Godin and he has written a book called *Permission Marketing*.

The associated issue is the legality of sending unsolicited e-
mails. The law varies from country to country. Clearly, if
your subscribers have asked to subscribe to your e-zine
(and you have proof of this), you are within the law. If you
are unsure of the current legal situation, seek legal
clarification (in the UK, you will need to refer to the Data
Protection Act).

Spam
'Spam e-mails' are unsolicited. They usually come from
people and organisations you have never heard of. Here is a

selection of products and services that have been offered via spam e-mail:

- Stocks and shares
- Free money, to use at a casino site
- Search engine placement services
- Computers
- A house in Austin, Texas
- Door handles from China
- A huge variety of get-rich-quick schemes

You can either delete spam or create a 'rule' to send any further messages from the same source directly to your Deleted folder.

A word of warning. If you reply to a spam e-mail (telling them to stop sending these messages), the sender will have verification of your e-mail address. It is highly likely that you will subsequently receive even more spam e-mails!

E-zine approaches

E-zine content falls into two main categories:

1 The straight sell
2 The relationship builder

Guess which one works best? Yes, it is relationship building. The way to achieve this is to write interesting, informative and useful e-zines. Give people tips and advice, similar to what they would read in a printed business magazine. Gradually, over a period of time, it is acceptable to mention your products or services. Nevertheless, if you go in for the kill too early you are in danger of switching off your readers.

Producing an e-zine is hard work. The reason that you might decide to produce one is because it works. Once you have set it up, all sorts of nice stuff can happen. Besides being a low cost way of regularly communicating with customers and prospects, e-zines can:

- Attract new visitors to your website
- Add value to your brand
- Create new revenue streams
- Help you to test new ideas, products, services and propositions
- Be used to target different messages to different groups

In addition, you will receive instant updates on any e-mail addresses which are now out of date. You will also receive fast feedback on what people like or do not like within your e-zine.

E-zine formats

You can choose to send your e-zines out in either plain text or in HTML format. The latter is also referred to as Rich Text. HTML is the computer language of the internet and it enables you to see graphics, colour and emphasis, such as emboldening.

However, many internet users still have problems receiving

and reading HTML e-zines. You may find that most of your readers would prefer to receive your e-zine in plain text format.

An alternative strategy is to offer both a plain text and an HTML version. This is fine, but it will make your life more complicated! Having said this, HTML allows the flexibility to present your e-zine in full colour and brilliantly displayed.

If you are starting up a new e-zine, ask your subscribers about the formatting issue (i.e. plain text or HTML).

Privacy please

You should advertise your e-zine on the homepage of your website. You will get more subscribers if you prominently display your privacy policy (see page 29).

Doing the writing

Although you are reading a book entitled *Writing Copy for the Web in a week*, you may not wish to produce all of the words yourself. If this is the case, here are some suggestions:

- You can recycle copy from other parts of your promotional mix. Take a look through your leaflets, brochures, website, press releases and direct mailshots.
- Another approach is to use a freelance copywriter. They usually charge per 1000 words. There are

many excellent freelancers – the issue is to find one with whom you get on and whose style you like. Because style is subjective, this may be the real challenge.

Your e-zine's very first words
The first word, right at the top of the e-zine, can be your choice of:

- Hi
- Hello
- Dear

Your choice is a matter of personal taste. Some people get around this issue by starting with the recipient's first name; however, this can be a little abrupt.

The second word should be the recipient's first name. This is possible through the use of e-mail list handling software (sometimes referred to as 'bulk e-mail handling software'). The key point is that nothing attracts someone's attention as much as their first name. You should find that response rates are higher if you use this method.

'From' lines
Ensure that your name (or your company's name) is stated in the 'From' line of your e-zine. This is all part of branding. These are the words which will appear in the recipient's inbox and so this is a very important detail.

'Subject' lines
Choose an e-mail list handling package that will allow you to enter a 'merge' field in the 'Subject' line of your e-zine

message. You can then merge the recipient's first name into the 'Subject' line. Using their first name is bound to get their attention.

The 'Subject' line is critical in e-mail marketing. Many people receive dozens of e-mails every day. The subject line acts like the headline within an advertisement. If it does not give a good reason to read on, the recipient is likely to delete the message there and then.

One tip is to try and use questions. As previously mentioned, when someone hears or reads a question, they inadvertently answer it. To prove this point, here are three questions for you: Do you drive a car? Are you a home owner? Is blue your favourite colour? What happened when you read them to yourself?

This little piece of psychology explains why so many advertisement headlines are structured as questions.

As an example of this approach, the 'Subject' line in a recent *Financial Times* e-zine read: 'Millions in unclaimed money. Is it yours?'

Another approach is to describe a promotional offer in the 'Subject' line. If it is relevant to the recipient, you may receive a surprising number of enquiries.

Here are a few ideas:

- Discounts, two-for-one offers, etc
- New information, which is now available on your website
- Downloadable e-books, articles or information
- Survey results

You have the choice of making these offers exclusive to your e-zine subscribers, or letting them tell other people. The best advice is to let them tell as many people as they want. When this happens in a big way (and it can), it is called 'viral marketing'.

Creating and testing new offers can be one of the most interesting and productive areas of e-marketing.

If you ask for money there and then, do not forget to have a hyperlink back to your website for secure on-line ordering.

The personal touch

When people first subscribe to your e-zine, try to send them a personal 'thank you' e-mail. You may want to take this a step further and visit their website (if they have one). You could write a few comments that lets them know that your message is not from a machine.

Unsurprisingly, you will receive great response rates to this approach. Here is an example from Stacy Markham in Canada:

> 'I was expecting a form confirmation, not an actual e-mail in return! You have been a great source of information and ideas. Can't thank you enough!
>
> Stacy

A few, personal, words of Web copy will connect with your new subscriber. You will be much more likely to keep them on your list, and this is the whole point, isn't it?

If you end up running a large scale e-zine, try to make your messages look as personal as possible.

The 'Unsubscribe' option

All of the reputable, professional e-zines should tell you how to unsubscribe from their circulation list. The unwritten rule seems to be to include this information somewhere near the top of your e-zine. Alternatively, the other location is right at the end, which is less convenient for the reader.

Putting it all together

Let's put these bits and pieces of advice together. This is how the words at the top of an e-zine could look:

Hi [First_Name]

Here is my next e-zine. To opt out, please reply with 'unsubscribe' in the subject line. This marketing e-zine is all about ways to build your business, using practical marketing ideas. It is aimed at businesses which market to other businesses.

IN THIS ISSUE:
- Goals, passion and strategy
- How to get free media coverage
- A favourite quotation
- Recommended website
- Book recommendation
- Request for help

As you can see, the e-zine is presented as a column of copy –
about 60 characters wide. This is to try and avoid oddly
wrapped text appearing on the recipient's screen. Do not try
and achieve this using carriage returns. Set the margin you
want in your word processor or bulk e-mail handling
software. Ensure that the 'word wrap' function is 'on'.

As previously mentioned, always give people the big
picture for what lies ahead. Hence: 'This marketing e-zine
is all about . . .'.

Notice that:

- There is an unsubscribe option – loud and proud!
- There is a bullet point menu list. Readers can scan
  these choices and decide whether they want to read
  any further.
- Short sentences are used.
- The writing style is perhaps a little informal. Think
  about your writing style and take a look back at
  Tuesday's chapter.

Ideas of e-zine content

- 'Thank you for joining'/'This is what to expect' (sent
  to all new subscribers)
- Special offers (only available to your e-zine
  subscribers)
- New products and services
- New articles on your website (provide a direct
  hyperlink)
- Company news

- Technical/professional news
- Mini case studies and links to the full version(s) on your website
- Cross-selling (e.g. telling readers about offers from other parts of your organisation)
- Events (such as trade shows and seminars)
- Competitions
- Trends/what's happening in your industry
- Chairperson's/managing director's column
- Most popular articles on our website
- Most popular articles from previous e-zines
- Surveys (i.e. you ask the questions)
- Survey results
- Mentions of recent press cuttings
- How to get free samples
- A link to the charity you support
- Recommended websites, books etc
- Book reviews
- Recommended products or services from other companies (where you get a commission for introducing them and/or they e-mail their customers and tell them about you)
- Favourite quotations
- Advertisements from third parties (once you have achieved a high circulation)
- Adverts for non-competing e-zines (which include a 'reciprocal advert' for your e-zine)
- Hints, tips, advice
- Statistics/facts
- Testimonial statements
- Contributed content from business partners/suppliers/contacts

- Links to partners' websites (ask them to link back to you)
- 'White papers' (i.e. discussion documents on a subject of current interest)
- Something to make your subscribers laugh (or at least smile)
- Rewards for recommending your company or e-zine to others
- Rewards for subscribing for a certain length of time (these 'rewards' do not have to include money or even physical gifts; they can be, for example, information products)
- Changes in your contact details
- Contact name(s), phone number(s), your website address (as a hyperlink), e-mail address; other contact information

If you are sending out e-zines produced in HTML, you can use:

- A search engine facility
- Graphics and colour, to make it all look nice

However, please bear in mind previous comments about the use of HTML within e-zines.

A classic structure for sales-orientated e-mails

1 Tell the readers what the principle benefit is
2 Explain what this benefit will do for them

3 Introduce additional benefits
4 Fill in the details
5 Provide proof or credibility (use testimonials)
6 Explain what will happen if they fail to act
7 Go over the benefits again
8 Tell them what to do next, with a sense of urgency

Here is an example e-mail to promote some marketing seminars. You will see how the points we have been discussing are used. Scan the headings to see the structure used.

Hi [First_Name]

We are thinking about launching a new series of seminars. They will focus on all the latest techniques. They will be packed with proven, step-by-step ideas and advice. Would you be interested in attending? If sufficient people respond, we will update you on locations and prices.

KEEP UP-TO-DATE
This is a great opportunity to keep up-to-date and to meet colleagues from other companies.

TESTIMONIAL FROM A PREVIOUS SEMINAR
'An excellent seminar. Relaxed, enjoyable and informative.'
Mike Boxwell, Littlefoot Ltd

BONUS E-MAIL FOLLOW UP
Following each seminar, you will receive an e-mail reminder of the key learning points. There will also be tips and hints, to add further value.

GUARANTEE
If you aren't happy, we will refund your money. No questions asked.

REMIND ME WHAT I GET AGAIN?
An intensive, fast-paced, fun seminar. A collection of proven strategies and techniques. A networking opportunity. A follow-up e-mail to give you even more ideas, as well as to jog your memory.

We have spent two decades developing and working on these techniques. They aren't complicated or expensive to implement (far from it). However, they do require that you give them a fair shot.

WHAT DO I DO NOW?
If you would like to attend these events, please send confirmation by e-mail.

Subsequent topics will include:

- Low cost marketing principles
- Telemarketing: how to start the call
- PR: how to get your name in print
- E-mail marketing – the latest thinking
- Writing effective marketing copy

E-zines take time to set up and manage, but what marketing technique doesn't? Nonetheless, they are well worth the effort and will deliver long lasting value. It is best to just get going. Start small and start learning. It could well grow to become one of your most effective promotional tools.

Summary

Today we have explored one of the most cost-effective forms of marketing available. We have considered different approaches and formats, several tips and ideas and a step-by-step approach to e-zine production.

Web copy vocabulary and grammar

Vocabulary

When it comes to vocabulary, the rule is to keep it plain and simple. Do not use a complicated word when a simple one will do. Try to avoid technical language. Do not write to impress, write to communicate clearly.

Jargon busting

Does your industry have its own terms and phrases? Most industries and professions do. Whenever you can, avoid using this terminology. You have no way of knowing who will be reading your Web copy. Write for the uninitiated and you will attract more visitors and on-line relationships.

Acronyms

Do you know what a TLA is? It stands for Three Letter Acronym. The internet is strewn with them, for example FAQ (Frequently Asked Questions).

Here is the Web copy rule: every time you use an acronym, tell the reader what it means. The clearest way to do this is to write the words in full, complete with leading capitals. Follow this with the acronym in brackets. For example:

> Frequently Asked Questions (FAQ)

Having done this, you are at liberty to use the TLA as often as you wish!

Superlatives

Do you use amazing superlatives when you write about your fantastic organisation? Many sales and marketing people do. Business people largely use the internet to gather information and too many superlatives and too much 'marketing speak' will turn people off.

It is quite possible to write compelling, strong Web copy that is not stuffed full of superlatives. If you follow this advice, your Web copy will feel more believable and will generate better results.

A number of studies have been done in this area. Web copy

that simply provides the plain facts scores better in terms of comprehension and credibility. The message is to turn the hype generator off, when writing web copy.

Spelling and spell checkers

Do not rely on spell checkers! By all means use them. Then print out your Web copy and read through it carefully. Refer to Saturday's chapter (page 91) for more tips and hints on editing.

Building your vocabulary

The best way to build your vocabulary is to read widely. If you are reading this book, you are probably the type of person who browses through many websites. You may also read a number of other business, technical or professional books. In addition, perhaps you read novels (the more challenging, the better!). Another great way to increase your word power is to do crosswords.

Attention-grabbing words
Too much hype will turn people off. However, you still need to arrest their attention. Used sparingly, the following words will help you to do this:

> Announcing; Benefit; Bonus; Choose; Claim; Discover; Dissatisfied; Easy; Eliminate; Exclusive; Fast/Fastest; Free; Free trial; Guarantee/Guaranteed; Help; Idea; Imagine; Improved; Introducing/Introductory; Learn; Look; Love; Money; New; Now; Offer; Opportunity; Proven; Sale; Save; Secret; Secrets; Select; Sensational; Special; Surprise; Today; Warning; Why; Win; You.

From this list, the single most powerful word is 'Free'.

A useful little idea, which can help when you are feeling stuck, is to create a file that contains attention grabbing words. You can then open the file, copy a selection of the words and start playing around with them. For example, using the above list, these headlines were created:

Learn more about our easy-to-use help service
Click here for a great money saving opportunity
Special offer for our e-zine subscribers!
Introduction our new and improved website

Try it out for yourself. It is surprisingly easy to produce attention-grabbing headlines and opening sentences.

Grammar

Does grammar matter on the World Wide Web? Surely, in the 21st century, anything goes? What do you think?

Most people would agree that grammar matters. The first reason being that a good grasp of grammar helps with clarity and understanding. If you mangle the sentences what you write and don't bother with punctuation and all that boring stuff then believe you me your world wide web words are going to be tough to understand. (Sorry. Got a little carried away there).

Grammar is the science of language. English grammar comprises a body of rules, which are learned at school. Fashion and accepted usage of language are dynamic.

However, the need to deliver a clear message will always be with us.

Syntax
The sequence of words in a sentence can change their meaning. For example:

> Free e-book for visitors with great ideas

Where are the great ideas? Within the e-book, or within the minds of the visitors? If you tend to write long sentences, you will be in greater danger of creating syntax problems.

The answer is to ensure that the words that are most closely related are grouped together.

Idiom
Idiom is the way in which people put things. People from different parts of world or different parts of a county phrase things in different ways. If you analyse what is being said, logic and grammar may not help you!

The problem is that you have grown up saying and writing things in a certain way. Unfortunately, others may have difficulty in understanding you. Ask someone who grew up in a different place to you to read your Web copy. If possible watch and listen to them. If they frown and stumble over your words, it may be an idiomatic issue.

Punctuation
Punctuation is an attempt to replicate the rhythm of speech when it is written down. Communication started with speech. It developed over several hundred thousand years.

The written word has only existed for a few thousand years.

Although there are many rules of punctuation, there will always be arguments about it. This is largely because people believe that the right way is the way that they were taught. All that really matters is that your Web copy is easy to read and that it conveys your intended meaning as clearly as possible. Good punctuation can help you to achieve this objective.

Here are some punctuation points, which are particularly relevant to Web copy. Please note that they are listed alphabetically.

Capitals in headlines
Web copy writers and designers use capitals for emphasis, particularly in headlines. The problem is that it is more difficult to read sentences in upper case. Look at the headlines in a newspaper – how do they handle this issue?

Colon (and a word about stab points)
Colons (:) are very useful within Web copy. They show that there is a list coming up:

- Here is my first point
- Here is my second point
- Here is my third point

Notice that there are no full stops at the end of each stab point. It is annoying to see a series of stab points, some of which have full stops and some of which do not.

Commas
A comma is the equivalent of a pause for breath. It allows the reader to take in one thought, before you move on to another. The problem with commas is that people use them in

different ways. For example, do you consider that it is acceptable to have a comma before the word 'and'? There are many Web copy writers who denounce this practice.

Nevertheless, if you read widely, and study the work of some of the best-known authors, you will find that many of them do this. You may prefer to avoid using commas in this way (the last sentence used them for effect).

Dash
There is usually a better alternative to a dash – if you stop to think about it. Many websites are festooned with dashes. This is sometimes because the Web copywriters have not punctuated thoughtfully.

Inverted commas
There are two uses for inverted commas on the internet. The first is to emphasise something. For example:

> Subscribe to our free 'e-zine'

In this case, use single apostrophes.

On the internet, HTML allows you to embolden words and change their colour. You may find that this is a more effective alternative to using inverted commas.

The second use for inverted commas is to indicate spoken words:

> "I was most impressed by the service," commented John Smith.

In this case, the most commonly accepted practice is to use double quotation marks. Also notice that the second set of inverted commas come after the comma. Whichever practice you choose to follow, be consistent throughout the website.

Leading capitals
As a general rule, avoid the indiscriminate use of capital letters within websites and e-zines. For example, the words 'Company' and 'Internet' do not require capitals. The only reason for writing 'Company' is to highlight the fact that you are talking about your company. However, there is a danger that this can seem pretentious. Whichever way you decide to go – be consistent!

Semicolon
The semicolon (;) is a useful and elegant punctuation. It provides a longer pause than a comma, yet it is not as final as a full stop. It is a useful way to divide up a series of items within a sentence (although you may be tempted to use bullet points instead).

Keep your company in the singular
Here is a final grammar tip. Whenever you mention your organisation within your Web copy, refer to it in the singular, i.e:

Treetops Terrific Tree Surgeons *has* launched a new root mulching service.

An easy way to remember this rule is that there is only one Treetops Terrific Tree Surgeons Limited.

Summary

Today, we have discussed the important subjects of Web copy vocabulary and grammar. The key point to remember is to use words to clearly communicate your meaning. A brief refresher in this area can make all the difference.

Web copywriting strategies and editing

Writing strategies

How do successful Web copywriters produce their words? Here are some useful strategies.

Schedule writing time

Schedule your Web copywriting time in your diary. Many professional writers start writing early in the morning. They give themselves targets to hit in terms of the number of words they want to produce each day. Having written for a couple of hours or perhaps all morning, they go and do something else.

Build a structure: then fill in the gaps

Take your website plan and select a section. For example, you might choose 'Company News'. Begin by writing down the relevant headlines and subheads. For example:

Company News
Expansion update

Because the brain works by association, every noun or action word links to other words. For example, take the word 'Expansion'. This might make you think of new offices, new markets and new services. Or perhaps it made you think of marketing and the latest advertising campaigns and press cuttings:

Company News
Expansion update
- New offices
- New markets
- New services
Marketing update
- Our latest ad campaign
- PR success

You may then think about people and create a 'People' section (complete with new staff, staff stories and an update on the training programme). An important person is the managing director – you could have a regular column for the MD. The list has now expanded to look like this:

Company News
Expansion update
- New offices
- New markets
- New services
Marketing update
- Our latest ad campaign
- PR success
People
- New staff
- Staff stories
- Training programme
Managing Director's column

By the way, this is exactly how this book was written. It started with chapter headings and then section headings. Then each section was written at a time. Have you heard the old joke:

Q: 'How do you eat an elephant?'
A: 'A plate at a time.'

Large tasks (or should that be tusks?) are overwhelming. If you break them down into little chunks, they are much more bearable.

Get into the habit of writing

Some Web copywriters find it difficult to produce the required words 'on demand'. If this sounds like you, try this approach:

> 1 List (or Mind Map®) the key points you need to get across
> 2 Give yourself a fixed amount of time to write what you can
> 3 Start writing about the first point – do not stop to think, just keep writing
> 4 Take a short break
> 5 Edit your work

This simple exercise should get you into the habit of writing. Once you have acquired this habit, you will find it gets progressively easier to sit down and produce those Web copy words!

Overcoming mental blocks

Mental blocks come in many shapes and sizes. It may be that you are not in the mood for Web copywriting. Maybe you cannot find the right approach or angle. Or you may not know where to start. Here are a series of ideas to help overcome mental blocks.

If you are looking for new ideas
- *Start an ideas scrapbook or file*: this might contain interesting articles that you want to refer to, forthcoming events that you want to tell your readers about or industry news.
- *Send out an e-mail*: perhaps to colleagues who have contributed in the past – asking for ideas and input.
- *Look at other websites*: see what they are writing about. It goes without saying that it is not a good idea to try using their words.
- *Try Mind Mapping*®: this is the thought-organisation technique made famous originally by Tony Buzan. It is a great way to generate ideas for your website. An example of a Mind Map® is on the following page.

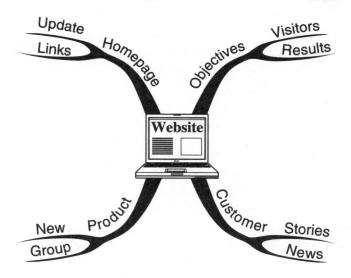

Please refer to *Mind Maps® in a week* by Steve Morris and Jane Smith.

Editing

Efficient editing can make all the difference to your Web copy. The first tip is to print it out. It is amazing how many changes you will spot, once you have done this. When you print out a lengthy piece of Web copy, in order to edit it, follow these stages:

> • Place the pages side by side on your desk.
> • Try to think of a better title (and, ideally, several alternative titles). After all, if the visitors do not like the title, they will not read any further.

- Consider whether you have packed enough benefits into the first few lines of the item (in order to tempt visitors to continue reading).
- Scan the headings and subheads. Imagine that you are a website visitor scanning the piece. Would you be interested enough to read the Web copy?
- Scan through the sections – look for anything you have repeated.
- Replace complicated words with simpler ones.
- Ruthlessly cut down sentence and paragraph length.
- Consider how you have used hyperlinks (are there any at all and where are they going?)
- Look at the end of the item – should there be a 'Call to action'?
- Are there any key points which you have left out?
- Make the necessary edits and then leave it alone (ideally, overnight).
- Ask someone else to give their opinion of it.
- Make the changes on-screen and leave it to simmer for a day or two; if you still like it when you return to it, you upload it to your website.

Cutting sentence length

Sentence length on websites can be very long. After 25 words or so, you can get lost! It is difficult to hold so many thoughts together as you read one long sentence after another.

If you examine any long sentence, you will see that it divides into separate thoughts. When you are editing, separate out the thoughts. These will be represented by key words or phrases. Once you hold these ideas in your head, the editing process is much easier. For example:

> This section of our website describes our products, which are used in the automotive industry.

The two key thoughts are 'products' and 'automotive industry'. On a website, I would cut this down to:

> Product information: Automotive industry

If that is a bit too brief for you, how about:

> We will now look at our automotive industry products.

Here is another example:

> We are well known for having a highly dedicated team that focuses on the customers' needs.

If you chop the sentence up into its constituent parts, you can make two short sentences:

> We have a highly dedicated team. We focus on your needs.

If in doubt, read the lengthy sentence out loud. You will hear where it breaks naturally. Punctuation is an attempt to make the written word represent the spoken word (with all its stops and starts).

Summary

Getting started and overcoming writer's block can be the real challenge for many Web copywriters. Today, we have examined various strategies to produce Web copywriting. Finally, we have considered the practical art of editing.

Web copywriting is a journey of discovery. By writing words for the internet, you will:

- Help your organisation to communicate with prospects and customers
- Become a better writer and increase your vocabulary
- Learn more about your subject matter
- Find out what your readers respond to
- Be part of a global communications revolution

We wish you every success with your Web copy!

The author

Nigel Temple BA (Hons) MCIM., is a marketing consultant, trainer, author and public speaker. He holds an honours degree in marketing and spent three years as a professional copywriter.

Nigel is the webmaster for two websites and has led numerous internet marketing seminars. He has advised companies of all sizes on internet marketing strategy, tactics, effectiveness and content. He trains some 2,000 marketing delegates a year.

Website: www.nigeltemple.com
email: nigel@nigeltemple.com
Tel: +44 (0) 1628 773128

SUN

MON

TUE

WED

THU

FRI

SAT

For information

on other

IN A **WEEK** titles

go to

www.inaweek.co.uk